LIKE

LIKE

A. E. STALLINGS

FARRAR STRAUS GIROUX

NEW YORK

Farrar, Straus and Giroux
120 Broadway, New York 10271

Printed in the United States of America
Published in 2018 by Farrar, Straus and Giroux
First paperback edition, 2019

The Library of Congress has cataloged
the hardcover edition as follows:
Names: Stallings, A. E. (Alicia Elsbeth), 1968– author.
Title: Like : poems / A. E. Stallings.
Description: First edition. | New York : Farrar, Straus and Giroux, 2018.
Identifiers: LCCN 2018010177 | ISBN 9780374187323 (hardcover)
Subjects: LCSH: Mythology, Classical—Poetry. | Families—Poetry.
Classification: LCC PS3569.T3197 A6 2018 | DDC 811/.54—dc23
LC record available at https://lccn.loc.gov/2018010177

Paperback ISBN: 978-0-374-53868-2

Designed by Quemadura

Our books may be purchased in bulk for promotional,
educational, or business use. Please contact your local
bookseller or the Macmillan Corporate and Premium Sales
Department at 1-800-221-7945, extension 5442, or by
e-mail at MacmillanSpecialMarkets@macmillan.com.

www.fsgbooks.com
www.twitter.com/fsgbooks
www.facebook.com/fsgbooks

3 5 7 9 10 8 6 4 2

For Jason and Atalanta

Contents

LIKE

After a Greek Proverb

Ουδέν μονιμότερον του προσωρινού

We're here for the time being, I answer to the query—
Just for a couple of years, we said, a dozen years back.
Nothing is more permanent than the temporary.

We dine sitting on folding chairs—they were cheap but cheery.
We've taped the broken windowpane. TV's still out of whack.
We're here for the time being, I answer to the query.

When we crossed the water, we only brought what we could carry,
But there are always boxes that you never do unpack.
Nothing is more permanent than the temporary.

Sometimes when I'm feeling weepy, you propose a theory:
Nostalgia and tear gas have the same acrid smack.
We're here for the time being, I answer to the query—

We stash bones in the closet when we don't have time to bury,
Stuff receipts in envelopes, file papers in a stack.
Nothing is more permanent than the temporary.

Twelve years now and we're still eating off the ordinary:
We left our wedding china behind, afraid that it might crack.
We're here for the time being, we answer to the query,
But nothing is more permanent than the temporary.

Ajar

The washing-machine door broke.   We hand-washed for a week.
Left in the tub to soak,   the angers began to reek,
And sometimes when we spoke,   you said we shouldn't speak.

Pandora was a bride—   the gods gave her a jar
But said don't look inside.   You know how stories are—
The can of worms denied?   It's never been so far.

Whatever the gods forbid,   it's sure someone will do,
And so Pandora did,   and made the worst come true,
She peeked under the lid,   and out all trouble flew:

Sickness, war, and pain,   nerves frayed like fretted rope,
Every mortal bane   with which Mankind must cope—
The only thing to remain,   lodged in the mouth, was Hope.

Or so the tale asserts—   and who am I to deny it?—
Yes, out like black-winged birds,   the woes flew and ran riot,
But I say that the woes were words,   and the only thing left was quiet.

Alice, Bewildered

Deep in the wood where things escape their names,
Her childish arm draped round the fawn's soft neck
(Her diffidence, its skittishness in check,
Merged in the anonymity that tames),
She knits her brow, but nothing now reclaims
The syllables that meant herself. Ah well,
She need not answer to the grown-up beck
And call, the rote-learned lessons, scolds and blames
Of girlhood, sentences to parse and gloss;
She's un-twinned from the likeness in the glass.
Yet in the dark ellipsis she can tell,
She's certain, that her name begins with "L"—
Liza, Lacie? Alias, alas,
A lass alike alone and at a loss.

Art Monster

My mother fell for beauty,
Although it was another species,
Ox-eyed, dew-lapped, groomed for sacrifice.

She had to devise another self
To put her self in—something inhuman
Or beauty could not possess her—

(O daedal mechanics!)
She grew huge with hybridity,
Rumor-ripened. I was born

To be amazed.
She fascinated me with cat's cradles,
Spun threads out of my hirsute

Hair shirt. I was fed
On raw youths and maidens,
When all I wanted was the cud of clover.

I was named after my step-
Father, dispenser of judgment,
No one called me my mother's son.

Minotaur, they said, O Minotaur,
You are unnatural, grotesque.
A hero will come to slay you, a hero

Who jilts princesses on desert islands.
It is heroic to slay, to break a heart,
To solve the archaic puzzle in the basement,

De-monster the darkness.
I await this patiently, as I bow to the yoke
Of making, scratching this earliest of inscriptions

On a potsherd, down here in the midden,
Writing left to right, then right
To left, as a broken beast furrows a field.

Autumn Pruning

FOR EVELYN

ET SPATIO BREVI SPEM LONGAM RESECES

You're doing them no favors
Letting them get too tall
Too fast for their own good;
Curtail the sprawl.

They'll only get leggy and weak
And die faster
If you don't take things in hand
And show them who's master.

Pretend you are that leveller,
The wind, unsheathe
Your blades—be the gnawing
Grazer's teeth.

Fall back, cluck the clocks:
The hour you're dreading
Comes with time on its hands
For the deadheading.

You water them and feed them
And call yourself a gardener.
You coddle and you pardon:
Be harder and hardener.

Battle of Plataea: Aftermath

Out of Book Nine of the Histories of Herodotus

◳

THE SPARTAN GENERALS

After the blood-brimmed field, we were amazed to stride
into those empty silken tents—bright tapestries, wrought
silver ornaments, the furnishings of solid gold. Eyes glazed
at all the untold booty: gods be praised! Our king bid for-
eign cooks spare no expense to make the meal our foes
would eat, prepare their pastries, spices, wine. Such slowly
braised flesh melting off the bone! Such colors, scents! Our
king laughed as he laid out on the cloth, beside the feast,
our ration of black broth: "Behold! They came to rob us of
our fare!" We also laughed, though fed up with that food,
the soldier's mess, the black broth of blood.

◳

We heard the Greeks had won. At once I went and decked myself with every bracelet, ring, gold necklace that I owned, and rouged my cheeks, and hastily had my maids arrange my hair. The other concubines slumped in despair; but I'd been snatched from Kos; my people, Greeks! Dressed in white robes of silk, we fled the tent, and drove through corpses, far as the eye could see, until I saw Pausanias, the king. I stepped with golden sandals through the gore, the lady that I was, and not the whore, and knelt, a supplicant, *Please set me free.* The roar of blood like silence in my ear, until: "Lady, arise, be of good cheer."

⌐

LAMPON THE AEGINITE

"Your glory after this victory is sealed," I told Pausanias, to please him. "Now crown it with revenge for Leonidas beheaded at Thermopylae. Remember the restitution that Xerxes denied us, and how he said Mardonius would pay it? Well, here is the cadaver—you just say it—and we'll impale Mardonius's head." He stood in silence as his face went somber. "Stranger," he addressed me, "on this field the crime was well avenged." As for that corpse, who knows what happened to it? There are versions—the truth is not so straight it never warps. Someone interred it—so I've heard it said—and reaped a handsome bounty from the Persians.

⌐

THE IMMORTALS

He called us the Immortals—the select companions who would battle at his side, Mardonius on his white charger. Pride, we felt, of course; maybe we half believed we were that day, not helmeted or greaved, no golden scales under the robes we wore. We wielded wicker shields for catching arrows. We were surrounded, as on mountain hunts a pack of Spartan hounds surrounds the boar. In that tight space, we knew our hopes were wrecked, like ships, frail bridges over Hellesponts, the horsewhipped waters bridling at the narrows. We were caught up in doom, as fish or sparrows, grateful like other men to die but once.

⌐

I lie here without honor, as I willed. Alone among those at Thermopylae I lived—if it is life to loathe each breath. They say I was the bravest Spartan here, but that I broke formation, and I fought not only as one not afraid of death, but one who seeks it, battle-mad, distraught. A Spartan soldier never leaves the line. It took so many Persians to get killed, I slogged on, drunk with slaughter as with wine. And when at last I met the foeman's spear, I laid my body down like shame, now free to fall amidst the dust, having fulfilled the ranks of the two hundred and ninety-nine.

Bedbugs in Marriage Bed

Maybe it's best to burn the whole thing down,
The framework with its secret joineries.
Every morning, check the sheets for blood
As though for tiny lost virginities,
Or murder itself distilled into a drop.
It might take lighter fluid to make it stop:
Maybe it's best to just give up and move.
Every morning, check the seem of seams.

Nothing for weeks, for months, but still you frown:
You still wake up at half past dawn each day
When darkness blanches and the stars go grey.
Who knows what eggs are laid deep in your dreams
Hatching like doubts. They're gone, but not for good:
They are the negatives you cannot prove.

Cast Irony

Who scrubbed this iron skillet
In water, with surfactant soap,
Meant to cleanse, not kill it,

But since its black and lustrous skin
Despoiled of its enrobing oils,
Dulled, lets water in,

Now it is vulnerable and porous
As a hero stripped of his arms
Before a scornful chorus.

It lacks
Internal consistency
As ancient oral epics

Where a Bronze Age warrior might appeal
To a boar's-tusk-helmet-wearing foe
Who has an anachronistic heart of steel,

Will of iron—from which metals
No one has yet forged a weapon,
Much less pans or kettles

(Though there must have been between
Two eras, awkward overlap
Enacted in the kitchen

When mother-in-law and daughter
Wrangled over the newfangled,
Over oil and water

In proverbial mistrust,
Brazen youth subject to iron age
As iron is to rust).

There can be no reasoning
With sarcastic oxygen,
Only a re-seasoning

Can give the vessel's life new lease:
Scour off the scab the color of dried blood,
Apply some elbow grease

To make it fast;
Anoint it, put it once more in the fire
Where everything is cast.

Colony Collapse Disorder

(Iliad, 2.87–2.90)

Just as a swarm pours from a hollow rock
In one long beeline for the wild thyme,
Alighting in clusters on this purple and that,
But is stricken with a mass amnesia
That disorients the compass of the sun,
And they forget the steps to traditional dances,
And each helicopters into a different dimness
Taking their saddlebags of sweetness with them,
And the hive goes dark, the queen is left to starve,
And the drones humbug the whimper of the world,
And the palace falls to ruins, broken into
By vandals who would loot the golden stores
Left in the brittle wax hexameters,
Just so . . .

The Companions of
Odysseus in Hades

After Seferis

Since we still had a little
Of the rusk left, what fools
To eat, against the rules,
The Sun's slow-moving cattle,

Each ox huge as a tank—
A wall you'd have to siege
For forty years to reach
A star, a hero's rank.

We starved on the back of the earth,
But when we'd stuffed ourselves,
We tumbled to these delves,
Numbskulls, fed up with dearth.

Crow, Gentleman

Pacing to and fro
Along the autumn shore
Among the wrack and reek

With your arms clasped behind your back
And sporting your grey frock coat
Trimmed in black

And your black hat and your lean long-legged stride,
Up and down the strand perusing
The headlines of the tide:

Casualties and statistics, futures, stocks,
The thousand natural shocks,
You clear your throat

Inspecting the ink-black seaweed tossed among the rocks
Like obsolete typewriter ribbons, rusty widow's weeds,
Scanning the flotsam for

Morsels cast up by the remorseless gossip of the sea's
Éminence grise,
How elegant you are, everyone concedes,

Gentleman Crow,
With your gimlet gaze, your sardonic beak,
How omnivorous, how sleek.

Life is a joke you crack,
Wry and amusing,
And death a dainty snack.

Cyprian Variations

A.

The heart is a divided city
Between two alphabets.
Church bells, minarets
Betoken
Time has stopped where it is broken.
Nothing forgets.
This is called history, not pity,
It is not spoken.

B.

To remember is to cross
Through no-man's-land
Into an imaginary country
You do not recognize
But where the streets are real, the walls
Are stone, you gaze through other eyes.

Γ.

The gaze scales the wall
And Love's promiscuous sparrows
Unyoked from her chariot
Cartwheel up against the sky and tumble
Pell-mell into the ghostly zone
Where the sandstone houses crumble,
And the unpicked, ripened dates
Fall to them alone.

Δ.

Within the walls we pass
The dying occupations of the past—
Last generations of vendors
Of woven stuffs, the menders
Of broken obsolete machines, of chairs,
Menders of soles, the last
Cobblers at their lasts.

Even the coffin maker is induced
To dread the mass-produced.

The Museum of Forgotten Trades
Brandishes its rusted blades
Sickles and ploughshares, blacksmiths' tools,
Instruments hang out of tune,
With spindles out of fairy tales,
Sharp enough to make a princess swoon,
And baskets to drain the whey from curdled milk.
In a flat brass pan,
Like the bandages of resurrected saints,
Wound up in dingy spools,
Lie the empty, light cocoons
Of the silkworm's silk.

Z.

In the marketplace I bought a sieve
Hand-hammered on a collar of wood
With nail holes patterned like a lacey flower—
It's understood
That it would make
A lovely powdered-sugar tracery on a cake,

A present you might give,

Keeping in your power

Something colder and more stark,

The way it lets the light sift through

The jagged holes,

The stars in shoals,

How it holds back the coarseness of the dark.

H.

We were told

That inside, under the library's stone dome

There was a poem, very old,

In characters of purest gold—

We could almost see

The arabesques of bright calligraphy,

But could not roam

Beneath that man-made firmament.

Should we be shocked

That it was locked?

Not knowing what it meant,

We could not read the poem, and we went.

Θ.

Two names for the nameless One, the father,
Though the ancient cult of the heart is another,
The dawn-star in the crescent,
The effervescent
Foam-born, the All Mother.

I.

By stages
Phallic talismans in picrolite
("The bitter stone")
Repeated through the ages
Evolve to female figurines
With outstretched arms
Or infants at the breast.
Grave goods, fertility charms—
They stand attentively behind vitrines
As if somehow human, warm,
And not schematic,
Cruciform.

K.

The mother says to her daughter:
The heart is an island.
To reach it,
You must cross salt water.
This is what the daughter fears:
That joy, like sorrow,
Must be reached by shipwreck,
Tossed on the flotsam of tears.

Λ.

Surfeit of the heart:
Every course
Brings more meat
And more remorse:
It chews what it must choose,
Impossible to refuse.

27

M.

The sky flies its banner, blue and white,
While military music sounds below:
Autonomy, says the heart, just so,
Is not the Yes of Night,
But the Day of No.

N.

There is another banner, white and red,
Not flying overhead,
But blazoned on the facing mountainside
As on a distant shore;
You wonder how it looked before
And are preoccupied.

Ξ.

In the heart of the island, in the mountains,
In the village where the pomegranate trees
Crack open their ruby lamps,

Soft and damp,
Night stoops swiftly and silently
As an owl's wings,
There in the heart, where it's cool and green,
And the source springs.

o.

An ancient bone-white vessel like an owl
Brims with delight,
Two eyes are holes, the work is fine—
For water, perfume, oil, or wine?
The mind wanders, though not far,
To another crepuscular fowl
We call the nightjar.

II.

I've never heard the nightingales of Platres,
Sleepless at the sill,
I never understood the odes and sonnets
That hymned that silvery trill;

29

The three-toned threnody that sounds the forest
Where I keep vigil still
Is not the Philomela of the poets
But poor Hank's whippoorwill.

P.

The insomniac
Has been here before. Her feet
Take her to the end of a barricaded street
Where a weary sentry
Forbids her entry,
And only cats and dreams
Pass to and fro across
The old acre of loss.
There is no way to get there now, it seems.

Σ.

You wander about
In the museum of confiscated saints
With their eyes scratched out,
Out of sight,

30

Pondering the quaint
Stubbornness of paint,
Saul blinded in the damask of the light.

T.

In this frame, St. George is still
Murdering the absurd
Ill-proportioned dragon,
That stands stock-still as if tethered,
Craning back its scrawny neck,
Brandishing its wings
Like an endangered bird,
Scarlet and irrelevant and feathered.

Υ.

From the ancient mosaic
The hound gazes up,
Adoring and agog,
Forever laying a partridge at your feet.
Beside her, someone has inlaid
Painstakingly in tesserae in Greek

31

"Fair Hunting," though the pup
Awaits something more prosaic,
Good dog.

Φ.

The dream
Gets up from its bed,
Arches its back, and stretches all its toes, very neat.
It crosses without passports
On padded feet
And curls up in another head
In another street.

x.

The insomniac weeps.
She's still awake.
Church bells rinse the air
With buckets of a bright
Clean music, and the urgent human cries
Of minarets punctuate the skies.
Hearing the day break and break
At last she sleeps.

The diptych icon's title:
Lady of Love, Lady of Sorrow.
The city stands
Beside herself, with love, with grief
Against a field of pure gold leaf
Cradling that sacred child
Tomorrow
In her hands.

Ω.

Rising from the sea
As on a foot-worn stair,
Rose-fingered dawn is scrubbing the light
Till it is raw and bare,
Sluicing away the night,
Calling us to prayer.

Denouement

Woolgathering afternoon:
All I've accomplished, all,
Is to untangle a wine-dark skein
And coil it into a ball.

I did not knit a swatch
For gauge—or cast a stitch—
Or pick a plausible pattern out,
I just unworked one hitch

After another, and went
Brailling along the maze,
Over, under, twist and turn,
To where the ending frays.

It's always best to leave
No glitches in the plot;
Sailors tell you that the yarn
Is weakest at the knot.

Open, do not tug
The little nooses closed,
Tease the cat from her cradle, lead
The minotaur by the nose

Out of the labyrinth
Through which all heroes travel,
And where the waiting wife will learn
To ravel's to unravel.

Out of the complicated,
Roll the smooth, round One,
So when it drops out of your lap
It brightly comes undone,

Leaping over the floor
Like swift ships outward-bound,
Unfurling the catastrophe
That aches to be rewound.

Dutch Flower Painting
from the 1670s

The ladybird (or -bug) exits stage right,
Or, no, stage left, tiptoeing the tabletop,
But somewhat towards us, towards the source of light;
While overhead, towers the scalloped cup

Of brindled tulip, pillowy peony,
Bouquet of blooms that never blew together,
Golden-age adynaton. The bee
That crawls away, behind the base, however,

As if to hide some sadness in its face,
Or disappointment in the painted bowers'
Stigma and stamen, vanishes apace
Behind what isn't there, that vase of flowers.

It doesn't fly. Is it an allegory?
It drumbles off to where oil's darkness hives,
Natura morta cum memento mori,
As by withdrawing, mystery survives.

Dyeing the Easter Eggs

Dyeing the Easter eggs, the children talk
Of dying. Resurrection's in the air
Like the whiff of vinegar. These eggs won't hatch,
My daughter says, since they are cooked and dead,
A hard-boiled batch.

I am the children's blonde American mother,
Who thinks that Easter eggs should be pastel—
But they have icon eyes, and they are Greek.
And eggs should be, they've learned at school this week,
Blood red.

We compromise, and some are yellow, or blue,
Or red and blue, assorted purples, mauves,
But most are crimson, a hematic hue,
Rubbed to a sheen with chrism of olive oil;
They will not spoil,

As Christian death is a preservative,
As Jesus trampled death and harrowed Hell.
The kids' palms are incarnadine and violet,
A mess! Go wash your hands! They wash their hands,
Punctilious as Pontius Pilate.

Eheu

After Horace

Ah, Postumus, arrived-too-late,
The years are running out.
Old age and death don't hesitate
Because you are devout:

Though altars groan with sacrifice,
Still you cannot deliver
Yourself from Pluto's heart of ice
Or from the dismal river

Where everyone must board the skiff
And everyone must cross,
Whether some poor working stiff
Or well-rewarded boss.

In vain, we run away from battle,
In vain, avoid the sea,
The treacherous sea, and autumn's rattle—
The wind won't let us be.

Someday you must lay eyes upon
The black, meandering waters,
And Sisyphus, who's never done,
And Danaus' wicked daughters,

And leave behind earth, house, and wife
Who only sought to please,
And all you planted in this life,
Save gloomy cypress trees.

Someday a more entitled heir
Will broach your cellar door
And swill the costly wine you spare
And stain your marble floor.

Empathy

My love, I'm grateful tonight
Our listing bed isn't a raft
Precariously adrift
As we dodge the coast guard light,

And clasp hold of a girl and a boy.
I'm glad we didn't wake
Our kids in the thin hours, to take
Not a thing, not a favorite toy,

And didn't hand over our cash
To one of the smuggling rackets,
That we didn't buy cheap life jackets
No better than bright orange trash

And less buoyant. I'm glad that the dark
Above us is not deeply twinned
Beneath us, and moiled with wind,
And we don't scan the sky for a mark,

Any mark, that demarcates a shore
As the dinghy starts taking on water.
I'm glad that our six-year-old daughter,
Who can't swim, is a foot off the floor

In the bottom bunk, and our son
With his broken arm's high and dry,
That the ceiling is not seeping sky,
With our journey but hardly begun.

Empathy isn't generous,
It's selfish. It's not being nice
To say I would pay any price
Not to be those who'd die to be us.

41

Epic Simile

FOR RACHEL HADAS

Right shoulder aching with daylong butchery,
Left shoulder numb with dints clanged on the shield,
The hero is fouled with blood, his own and others',
First slick, then sticky, then caked, starting to mat
His beard—the armor deadweight all around him;
His teeth grit and rattle with every jolt
Of bronze-rimmed wheels behind the shit-flecked horses.
But when he glimpses the mountains, the distant snow,
A blankness swoons upon him, and he hears
Nothing but the white vowels of the wind
Brushing through stands of spears like conifers
While a banner slips its staff and hangs in the blue
Like a kestrel or a contrail. The hero's death,
The prize, elusive quarry of his life,
Stands stock-still in her cloven tracks in snow
And turns, one ear tuned to the creek's far bank,
One dished towards him. Her unstartled gaze
Beads on him like a sniper's sights, until

At the clean report of a cracking poplar branch,

She leaps away like luck, over rapid water,

And snowfall scrims the scene like a mist of tears,

Like a migraine, like sweat or blood streaming into your eyes.

The Erstwhile Archivist

The summer that I turned nineteen
And felt grown-up in love,
I took a job as an archivist
Sifting through a trove

Of photographic negatives
From old insurance claims
And portrait studios: a million
Faces sans the names,

The white tire-marks of mangled cars,
Rooms washed away with fire
Or crisp with flood, and then the odd
Event like the premiere

Of *Gone with the Wind*—we had to file
Each image we could see
Under person, place, or thing—
Were accidents all three?

Sometimes we sleeved stale evidence:
The body's silhouette
Haloed on a motel floor
Near a lit cigarette.

And then there were the wedding shots—
I catalogued each groom
Arrayed in tailored light, each grey-haired
Bride in weeds of gloom,

Her irises were milky, blind,
Her gaze was like a hole,
The roses in her hand were ash,
Her diamond ring was coal.

But these were just the revenants,
The brittle shades of love,
I lifted like X-rays to the light
In a pale latex glove,

The summer I turned archivist,
And filed the past away
For some frown-lined researcher
On some far winter day.

First Miracle

Her body like a pomegranate torn
Wide open, somehow bears what must be born,

The irony where a stranger small enough
To bed down in the ox-tongue-polished trough

Erupts into the world and breaks the spell
Of the ancient, numbered hours with his yell.

Now her breasts ache and weep and soak her shirt
Whenever she hears his hunger or his hurt;

She can't change water into wine; instead
She fashions sweet milk out of her own blood.

For Atalanta

Your name is long and difficult, I know.
So many people whom we didn't ask
Have told us so
And taken us to task.
You too perhaps will wonder as you grow

And blame us with the venom of thirteen
For ruining your life,
Using our own love against us, keen
As a double-bladed knife.
Already I can picture the whole scene.

How will we answer you?
Yes, you were in a hurry to arrive
As if it were a race to be alive.
We weighed the syllables, and they rang true,
And we were hoping too

You'd come to like the stories
Of princesses who weren't set on shelves
Like china figurines. Not allegories,
But girls whose glories
Included rescuing themselves,

Slaying their own monsters, running free
But not running away. It might be rough
Singled out for singularity.
Tough.
Beauty will be of some help. You'll see.

But it is not enough
To be nimble, brave, or fleet.
O apple of my eye, the world will drop
Many gilded baubles at your feet
To break your stride: don't look down, don't stoop

To scoop them up, don't stop.

Glitter

All that will remain after an apocalypse is glitter.

—British *Vogue*

You have a daughter now. It's everywhere,
And often in the company of glue.
You can't get rid of it. It's in her hair:
A wink of pink, a glint of silver-blue.
It's catching, like the chicken pox, or lice.
It travels, like a planetary scar.
Sometimes it's on your face, or you look twice
And glimpse, there on your arm, a single star.
You know it by a hand's brushing your neck—
You blush—it's not desire, not anymore—
Just someone's urge to flick away the fleck
Of borrowed glamour from your collarbone—
The broken mirror Time will not restore,
The way your daughter marks you as her own.

Half of an Epic Simile
Not Found in Hesiod

As at the winter solstice, when a faded blonde
On the brink of middle age goes to the salon
To brighten up her outlook and her spirits
(Warm water on her scalp, the rich shampoo
That breathes of almond blossoms), to submit
To another's expert disinterested caresses,
While outside the plate-glass window, people push
Against the dwindling year, and lean into
The wind, their foreheads pinched with doubt and debt,
And it's afternoon, but night comes chattering down
Like the shutters of a shop in a recession,
And all she asks for is a color adjustment,
For rays of honey to eclipse the grey,
And for the light to lengthen just a little.

The Last Carousel

The horses have seen better days go by
With the one eye that peers
Out on the orbiting world. The other eye

Has always looked inward, to where the moving parts
Are hidden by a column of gilt-edged tarnished mirrors.
Why are we pierced through our hearts

By their poles of polished brass?
Mismatched orphans, some antique,
Carved of solid wood, some factory-molded fiberglass,

They course counterclockwise, round and round,
While Time holds them at arm's length.
Their feet are shod but never touch the ground.

They've known the shake of reins bidding them race,
The heels that drum their flanks
Urging them faster and faster in one place,

The laughter and the outside voices calling,
The tinned music stuttering in its rut,
The last seasick tide rising or falling.

Their gallop is a wave that seizes.
In their rhythmic progression, they are cousin to the horses
On stolen, marble friezes,

In bas-relief, in some far-off museum,
That once were prinked with paint.
But now that I see them

Waiting patiently beneath the hive of garish light,
As one giddy generation mounts,
And another sulks into the night—

One last go, it isn't fair!—
I am moved by the pivot of their stillness,
By their ragged comet tails of genuine horsehair.

Lice

It starts with a hunch:
watching her scratch unthinking-
ly behind her ear.

You wiggle a hitch
loose along a burnished shaft.
It's just as you fear:

now you're picking nits
with a fine-toothed comb no less,
lousy metaphor.

How pediculous!
But now it's personal, it's
chemical, it's war,

no quarter, no truce.
You lord it over their dead,
their pedantic puce,

undo the unborn
(murder is meticulous)
that star her dark head,

divide in sectors,
lest anything be over-
looked, doubt's niggling itch.

Mankind will never
be rid of them; like the poor
they're always with us:

vectors of nothing
but disgrace and shame, charmless
as they are harmless.

Like, the Sestina

With a nod to Jonah Winter

Now we're all "friends," there is no love but Like,
A semi-demi-goddess, something like
A reality-TV-star look-alike,
Named Simile or Me Two. So we like
In order to be liked. It isn't like
There's Love or Hate now. Even plain "dislike"

Is frowned on: there's no button for it. Like
Is something you can quantify: each "like"
You gather's almost something money-like,
Token of virtual support. "Please like
This page to stamp out hunger." And you'd like
To end hunger and climate change alike,

But it's unlikely Like does diddly. Like
Just twiddles its unopposing thumbs-ups, like-
Wise props up scarecrow silences. "I'm like,
So OVER him," I overhear. "But, like,
He doesn't get it. Like, you know? He's like
It's all OK. Like I don't even LIKE

Him anymore. Whatever. I'm all like . . ."
Take "like" out of our chat, we'd all alike
Flounder, agape, gesticulating like
A foreign film sans subtitles, fall like
Dumb phones to mooted desuetude. Unlike
With other crutches, um, when we use "like,"

We're not just buying time on credit: Like
Displaces other words; crowds, cuckoo-like,
Endangered hatchlings from the nest. (Click "like"
If you're against extinction!) Like is like
Invasive zebra mussels, or it's like
Those nutria things, or kudzu, or belike

Redundant fast-food franchises, each like
(More like) the next. Those poets who dislike
Inversions, archaisms, who just like
Plain English as she's spoke—why isn't "like"
Their (literally) every other word? I'd like
Us just to admit that's what real speech is like.

But as you like, my friend. Yes, we're alike
How we pronounce, say, "lichen," and dislike
Cancer and war. So like this page. Click *Like*.

Little Owl

(Athene noctua)

It's not what we see, but what sees us
Makes us who we are.
Do you remember years ago on Spetses,
Under the evening star,
As the surf rolled and rolled on its glass dowel
We strolled along the sea road
And spied a little owl
Less a bird
Than a small clay jar
Balanced implausibly on an olive branch,
A drab still vessel attuned to whatever stirred,
Near or far:
Hedgehog shuffling among windfall of figs,
Gecko, mouse.
Then she swiveled the orbit of her gaze upon us
Like the Cyclops eye-beam of a lighthouse.

Lost and Found

I crawled all morning on my hands and knees
Searching for what was lost—beneath a chair,
Behind the out-of-tune piano. *Please*,
I prayed to Entropy, let it be there—
Some vital Lego brick or puzzle piece
(A child bereft is hiccoughing despair),
A ball, a doll's leg popped out of its socket,
Or treasures fallen through a holey pocket.

II

Amazing what webbed shadows can conceal—
A three-wheeled Matchbox car, or half a brace
Of socks or shoes. Oblivion will steal
Promiscuously—lost without a trace,
Microscopic bits of Playmobil,
The backup set of house keys. You misplace
Your temper and your wits, till you exhaust
All patience with the hours it has cost.

III.

I thought too of that parable, the other—
Not the one men preach of the lost sheep,
The lesser-known one, on the housewife's bother
Over a missing coin: how she must sweep
The house to find it. No doubt, *she* was a mother,
I think, and laugh, and then I want to weep:
The hours drained as women rearrange
The furniture in search of small, lost change.

IV.

"Tidy up your room," I told my son,
"That way, it's easier to look." (It's true.)
He made an effort, a halfhearted one
Abandoned after just a block or two.
"It isn't fair," he said, "it isn't fun,
I never do what *I* would like to do,
But you, you always do *just what you want*."
Which plucked a string, as though a cosmic taunt.

V.

I paused. "Is *that* what you think, then," I said.
(Sometimes he seemed less seven-year-old boy
Than teenager.) "That making you go to bed
Or washing dishes is something I *enjoy*,
And that I've nothing better to do instead
Of hunting for a crappy plastic toy?"
Raised voices, tears, apologies all round,
And yet the crucial piece was never found.

VI.

That night I was still seeking in my dreams,
Still groping after fragments and the maimed,
Just as in dreams a seamstress stitches seams,
Or politician spins truth unashamed,
Or, loping through remembered fields and streams,
The hound pursues the scent that can't be named,
Her paws a-twitch, though heavily she lies,
And dogsbody the body does not rise,

VII.

Or as a poet stalks a skittish rhyme
Behind her lidded eyes, beneath the mask
Of sleep—because the mind has no free time
But keeps at night to its diurnal task
And pushes the stone as high as it can climb
Before it trochees down again. Don't ask
The mind to rest, though someday it must cease;
In life, only the flesh has any peace.

VIII.

It seemed I searched, though, in a dusty place
Beneath a black sky thrilled with stars, ground strewn
With stones whose blotting shade seemed to erase
The land's gleam (like a tarnished silver spoon);
A figure neared, with adumbrated face,
Who said, "This is the valley on the moon
Where everything misplaced on earth accrues,
And here all things are gathered that you lose."

IX.

The moon? Yet I did not dispute the claim.
She seemed familiar—hard to tell among
Such alien surroundings. All the same,
A word seemed out of reach, tip of my tongue,
Close-clustered consonants and vowels, a name.
Beneath her hood I glimpsed a face not young
But elegant, refined as it grew older.
My name she knew, although I hadn't told her.

X.

Now that my eyes had focused in the dark
I saw that what seemed mountains, ridges, hills
All hemmed around us, flinging down their stark
Chill silhouettes, were overflowing landfills,
Huge heaps of congeries. And I could mark
The mounds of keys or orphaned socks, dropped pills
(Those were the things that I could recognize),
Like bombed-out cities black against the skies.

XI

Somehow it brought to mind the vestibule
Jumbled with hats, umbrellas, backpacks, totes,
Scarves, gym shoes, that they keep at my son's school
Behind the lunchroom: bins of winter coats,
Hairbands, sunglasses stacked up on a stool—
Each thing spoke volumes or quipped anecdotes—
Lorn, makeless gloves; lunch boxes starting to mottle.
(I'd come to seek an AWOL water bottle.)

XII.

"Look there," she said, and gestured to the keys,
"Those are the halls to which we can't return—
The rooms where we once sat on others' knees,
Grandparents' houses, loving, spare, and stern,
Tree houses where we whispered to the trees
Gauche secrets, virgin bedrooms where we'd burn,
Love's first apartments. As we shut each door,
It locks: we cannot enter anymore."

XIII.

There was a mound that loomed above our heads,
A skein of dusty strands large as a barn.
"Are these," I asked, "the sum of hair one sheds
In life, or all the rips one has to darn?"
She laughed and said, "Those are the frayed, lost threads
Of conversations, arguments, the yarn
Of thought and logic's clews we'd thought we'd spun
Only to find they'd somehow come undone."

XIV.

Then there was sunk, among the hills, a bowl,
A wide, shallow depression, in which "O"s
Or ciphers gathered, thin, and black as coal,
Like washers of black iron. I asked, "And those?"
"They mark our absences—it's through the hole
Of lapsed attention that the moment goes."
I thought of those assemblies with repentance
Where I had mocked the prizes of attendance.

XV

"And that?" I pointed to a pyramid
Of papers, ever threatening to tumble.
It shifted—sheaves of pages suddenly slid
Then seemed to settle. I stepped back from the jumble,
Thinking we might be buried there amid
An avalanche of foolscap. A hushed rumble
Shuffled its menace. I whispered, "Then are those
The poems lost, or pages of sure prose—

"Maybe even something that would sell
(A book about a young aspiring warlock?)—
That disappeared when something broke the spell,
When toddler learned to work the study door-lock,
Or telephone brayed bad news—or the front bell
Portended importunity from Porlock?"
"The poems," she said, "that perish at the brink
Of being, aren't so many as you think,

XVII.

"Nor yet so great. No, no, these are the letters
We meant to write and didn't—all the unsaid
Begrudged congratulations to our betters,
Condolences we owed the lately dead,
Love notes unsent—in love, we all are debtors—
Gratitude to teachers who penned in red
Corrections to our ignorant defenses,
Apologies kept close like confidences."

XVIII.

A vague, headachy cloud among the towers
Rose, as heaps of grey down from black swans.
"Those are," she said, "Insomnia's desperate hours,
Lost sleep: countdown of clocks, the impotent yawns;
The teething cries, sweet drowsiness that sours,
The night feedings that soldier into dawns."
I watched as creatures, etiolated, pale,
Weighed bales of feathers in a brazen scale.

XIX.

What were the creatures doing? She explained,
"For every hour that we lose of sleep,
Another hour of wakefulness is gained;
There is a tally that we have to keep."
"Unbearable minutes!" She saw that I was pained.
"Perhaps," she said, "but sometimes in the deep
Of night, reflections come we cannot parse—
To *consider* means to contemplate the stars."

XX.

Skittering round us, skirls of silver sand
Would swarm and arch into a ridge or dune,
And then disperse, as if an unseen hand
Swept them away (there was no wind), then soon
Accumulate elsewhere, a sarabande
Of form and entropy, a restive swoon
Of particles, forever in a welter,
Like starling murmurations seeking shelter.

XXI

"The sands of Time." (I didn't have to speak;
She answered straightaway with some disdain.)
"With scything hands you hasten through the week
Clockwise, while widdershins, the fair hours drain.
Haste," she declared, "is Violence, in Greek."
Then she bore on in silence once again.
"Why won't they rest?" I asked in puzzlement.
"Minutes are not lost," she said, "but spent."

XXII.

Nearby, a glint of vitreous splinters, foiled
With silver, bristled in a jagged mass.
"This is a woman's loveliness that's spoiled
With age," she said, "and tears, and days that pass—
Her raiment that is creased, thread-worn, and soiled.
Here, seek that vanished beauty in this glass."
And gave me a reflection where I sought her—
Nothing at first—but then I saw my daughter—

XXIII

Eyes brown, not blue; the hair, not straight, but curled.
"Not truly lost," she laughed, at my surprise.
"Some things fetch up on the bright shores of the world
Once more, under a slightly different guise;
Meanwhile, they are not lost, but somehow furled
Back in the heart of things from which they rise."
And saying this, she turned, and did not wait,
But something nearby made me hesitate,

XXIV.

I couldn't make it out at first: a pile
Of bone chips, ivory splinters? Like a sleuth,
I sneaked a handful, following the while,
But stopped short when I realized the truth,
And let them fall, and dropped my neutral smile:
Each keen point was a tiny human tooth.
I looked back over my shoulder for a glimpse
And gasped to see a thousand small, grey imps

XXV

Go scampering up the hill, with wrinkled wings
Leathern like bats, with backs hunched up to carry,
Slung on their shoulders, sacks bulged with grim things—
More teeth, I thought—remains you ought to bury.
My guide observed me watch their scurryings.
"But don't you recognize a real tooth fairy?
Each baby tooth, deciduous but bright,
Stands for a childhood rooted in delight,

XXVI.

"But those that come here stained, starting to rot,
Are childhoods that are eaten up with sorrow,
Eroded by the acids of their lot,
And others' sins they are compelled to borrow."
"So many!" I exclaimed, as fairies brought
More chatterings of teeth. "Yes, and tomorrow,
It never stops. Each childhood is outgrown
By sharper permanence. Even your own"

XXVII

(Children, she meant) "cannot stay as they are.
Already, your son's childhood is consigned"—
She held up six fine milk teeth in a jar—
"Already he is leaving it behind,
Striding forth as light strides from a star;
And though the star blow out, inert and blind,
The light strides on, and reaches other eyes
That in some distant time scan these same skies."

XXVIII.

At last our path came to a spring whose gleam
Provoked my thirst. Two cups of battered zinc
Hung from a pair of hooks there: one had "Dream"
Inscribed upon it; on the other, "Think."
But when I dipped each cup's lip to the stream,
Immediately it began to sink.
When both had vanished, she said, "Do not wet
Your lips here with the waters of Forget."

XXIX

Not water, though, I knew as I drew near it—
It was a liquid, true, but more like gin
Though smelling of aniseed—some cold, clear spirit
Water turns cloudy. "Many are taken in,
Some poets seek it, thinking that they fear it,
The reflectionless fountain of Oblivion.
By sex, by pills, by leap of doubt, by gas,
Or at the bottom of a tilting glass.

XXX.

"But you, you must remember, and return,"
Now I saw clearly skin of alabaster,
Her moon-washed hair, a gaze one could discern
As gunmetal grey—and then at last I asked her,
"Who are you? Are you She who used to burn
With sweetbitter eros? Or She who learned to master
The art of losing? She who did dying well,
Beekeeper's waspish daughter? Amherst's belle?"

XXXI

"Don't you know? But everyone who loses
Has prayed and laid an offering at my shrine—
Though each who knows me calls me as she chooses,
My name's Mnemosyne; I am divine.
I am," she said, "the Mother of the Muses—
Imagine, you have two, but I have nine!
More even than that—for all the arts that be,
Sciences too, are born of Memory."

XXXII.

It made me smile, to think of her at her loom,
A gaggle of teenaged daughters at her feet:
No-nonsense Clio, Melpomene gothed in gloom,
Graceful Euterpe, Terpsichore, who won't eat,
Polyhymnia, with incense for perfume,
Thalia, laughing, Urania taking a seat
At the telescope, Erato fine-tuning her fiddle,
Calliope starting her story in the middle.

XXXIII.

She led the way now through a garden of musks
From dark, fanged flowers—incarnadine, maroon.
We came upon two gates: one made of tusks
Of prehistoric elephants, one hewn
From massive, savage horns. All round, the husks
And bones of great extinctions had been strewn.
"Here we must pass," she said, "but not together.
You pass through one; I shall go through the other."

XXXIV.

Then something began to happen. I felt her arm
On mine, we seemed to travel, standing still,
I saw a light. Had someone come to harm?
I heard a distant siren, pulsing, shrill—
But then I recognized the old alarm
Harping on its monitory trill—
It's Dawn again, come with her golden rule
Like a shepherd's crook, to harry us to school.

XXXV.

There are lunches to make, I thought, and tried to find
Some paperwork from last week I'd mislaid
(Due back, no doubt, today, dated and signed),
Instead, unearthed a bill we hadn't paid,
Located shoes, a scarf, a change of mind:
I tried to put aside mistakes I'd made,
To live in the sublunary, the swift,
Deep present, through which falling bodies sift.

XXXVI.

I saw the aorist moment as it went—
The light on my children's hair, my face in the glass
Neither old nor young; but bare, intelligent.
I was a sieve—I felt the moment pass
Right through me, currency as it was spent,
That bright, loose change, like falling leaves, that mass
Of decadent gold leaf, now turning brown—
I could not keep it; I could write it down.

Memorial (*Mnemosyno*)

You'd lost your father's grave.
We wandered row by row and plot by plot.
And it was hot
Under stiff cypress shade, the stillness drowned
By a lone insect's corrugated sound.

You went on ahead
To inquire of the bureaucracy of the dead.
Overdressed, uncomfortable as guilt,
We stood around, not knowing how to behave.
The kids began to wilt,

And there was nowhere to sit that wasn't a tomb.
Each grave was kitted out
With a dustpan and a little broom
To tidy the garden beds of the bereft,
And here and there hung plastic watering cans

Chained to headstones and trees—without a doubt,
Even in this place, there was a problem with theft.
Then you came back
With the coordinates, and snagged a priest
Glistening in polyester black,

Who, at the grave, now found,

Spoke of the rest and rising of the dead

As if they were so many loaves of bread

Tucked in their oblong pans

In a kitchen gold with sunlight, rich with yeast.

Momentary

I never glimpse her but she goes
Who had been basking in the sun,
Her links of chain mail one by one
Aglint with pewter, bronze, and rose.

I never see her lying coiled
Atop the garden step, or under
A dark leaf, unless I blunder
And by some motion she is foiled.

Too late I notice as she passes
Zither of chromatic scale—
I only ever see her tail
Quicksilver into tall grasses.

I know her only by her flowing,
By her glamour disappearing
Into shadow as I'm nearing—
I only recognize her going.

The Mycenaean Bridge

Beside the culvert of cement,
Beside the ill-made potholed modern road,
The cyclopean boulders hold their poise
And the keyhole of the corbelled arch
Bears their load.

Atop, goat droppings tell
That it is still in use, at least for goats,
This bridge that shouldered soldiers on the march,
And chariots, and harvest-laden carts
Over the sudden moats,

The torrents of the rainy equinox.
Now from its centuries-dark archway pour,
And back again there dive,
A host of stings: the sweetness-hoarding
Wild black bees. They hive

Here in the hollow in the rocks
Upon which leans the bridge,
And gather gold dust for their queen
Out over hills pockmarked with looted tombs,
Across aeons that span from ridge to ridge.

The Myrtle Grove

FOR R.W.

1.

I would not like to think your soul abides
In some grey wasteland of the suicides
Who, loathing the light, have flung their lives away,
And innocent, condemned themselves to stay
In the shadow of the act that, now it's done,
They would exchange for one peep at the sun,
Though life were toil and trouble. The swamp of hate
Encircles them; their path is barred by fate.

I'd rather think you found yourself instead
Among the moon-dim ladies of the dead—
Phoenician Dido's solemn sisterhood—
Who wander in that dark-leaved, fragrant wood
Sacred to Venus—in the myrtle grove
Where dwell the shades of those who died for love.

Last night I dreamt about the suicide
With her water-colored eyes, her ashen hair.
She didn't ask what I was doing there
Lucubrating on the other side.
(In dreams, it's curious how you decide—
Though every character is child and heir
To your waking self—that they are real, and their
Voices aren't just echoes from inside.)

She said she wanted to give me a tattoo
Here on my chest—she said it was a heart—
Though it was crowned with antlers like a hart,
Its legend, *Whoso list*; but I said no.
She turned as if to say how could I know
What stops the heart's tattoo, the heart's tattoo.

Night Thoughts

Night thoughts are not like bats,
Do not trip out at dusk
With bumbershoots and spats,
And fur coats, in sub fusc,

Do not fall into flight
Into the upside-down
Colander of the night,
And stagger on the town.

They do not zag and zig
Giddy on the wing
As a jigsaw's jig.
They do not squeak or sing.

They're not the sharps and flats,
The blue notes in the key,
The way it seems that bats
Are accidentals, free

To swoop beyond the tune.
The thoughts at night that come
Are midnight's afternoon,
Desolate and dumb.

They weep their limestone tears,
They hang, but do not fly,
Accretion of the years,
They sweat. They petrify.

Pandora

It was the Iron Age. The men had been drinking,
Those two surly brethren, Hindsight and Forethought.
They sent her down to the cellar to fetch more booze
Even though she'd murmured, "You've both had enough."

Forethought, at least, you'd think would eschew a hangover.
But then he was always cocky: he'd filched sparks
From the gods, and hadn't foreguessed, nickname aside,
The prank would backfire. His liver hadn't yet

Begun to creak as if an eagle tore it each morning.
Hindsight, her husband, of course remorsed their marriage.
He'd said she was a punishment from Zeus,
And that virginity made for a sorry dowry

Depreciating soon as you drove it off the lot.
There was just a dram in the drained keg, and that
She thought she'd drink herself, dregs be damned.
Broach a new cask? They were huge, a fathom tall,

A man could drown in them, set deep in the floor,
So you could reach the mouth. She pried open
The charactered seal with only her grappling fingers,
But the wine had vinegared, or worse. What fumes!—

Acrid, with notes of brimstone. Flies belched out.
Hindsight would give her "what for" tonight for sure.
Ouch: just then the baby gave a disgruntled kick
Right behind where she would have had a belly button

If she'd been born, instead of just made up by poets.
Hindsight hankered for sons, more braces of hands
For his failure of a farm. But if it were a daughter,
She'd have some company, and name her Heather maybe, or Hope.

Parmenion

Athens

The air-raid siren howls
Over the quiet, the un-rioting city.
It's just a drill.
But the unearthly vowels
Ululate the air, a thrill

While for a moment everybody stops
What they were about to do
On the broken street, or in the struggling shops,
Or looks up for an answer
Into the contrailed palimpsest of blue.

Always we forget. It's once a year
Just as lush September's getting sober
Ambushed by October.
It strikes the heart like fear, as the vibrations build
To an All Clear.

The test is dubbed "Parmenion"
After the general second in command
To Alexander,
Implicated by his own son
In a confession to a plot of treason.

And Alexander had him killed,
Old family friend, right-hand man, comrade in arms,
Probably without reason.
A pity.
Hence the groundless wails, the false alarms.

Peacock Feathers

A plague of feral peafowl in the garden
(I know—who knew?) now decimates the grapes,
Makes salad of the young geraniums—
Dustups of dust baths in denuded planters!
They leave ubiquitous piles of poo, as drab
As any other poo. They make that sound
As if of something throttled in the jungle,
Or honk to out-goose geese. They're worse than roosters
At judging dawn—say four a.m.—the moon
When full, rattles them off, one after the other.
They're something else to fight about: you swear
Come autumn, you'll take up a rifle—blam!
Are we the sort who murder birds? Sometimes
They catch us off guard with pure pulchritude,
The sheer implausibility of it,
Sublime unlikelihood. And when they molt,
The garden sprouts a ferny iridescence
Dazzled with targets. Sometimes I think of Argus,
Monster with a myriad sleepless eyes
Set to spy on Jove or ward his mistress,

Fabled insomnia of the suspicious spouse.
Her pet slain, Juno gathers the glamour of glares,
Still watchful, in a fan of green-blue feathers—
Unlucky things to bring into the house.

Pencil

Once, you loved permanence,
Indelible. You'd sink
Your thoughts in a black well,
And called the error, ink.

And then you crossed it out;
You canceled as you went.
But you craved permanence,
And honored the intent.

Perfection was a blot
That could not be undone.
You honored what was not,
And it was legion.

And you were sure, so sure,
But now you cannot *stay* sure.
You turn the point around
And honor the erasure.

Rubber stubs the page,
The heart, a stiletto of lead,
And all that was black and white
Is in-between instead.

All scratch, all sketch, all note,
All tentative, all tensile
Line that is not broken,
But pauses with the pencil,

And all choice, multiple,
The quiz that gives no quarter,
And Time the other implement
That sharpens and grows shorter.

Placebo

No can do. I am
doctor not of medicine,
but Latinity.

I am the future,
singular, indicative.
The first person. What

do you take me for?
If is a real condition.
If I'm a pill, then

you are double blind.
What you don't know can't hurt you.
Spoonful of sugar,

it's all in your head,
this dendritic alchemy
of pain. Nothing works.

Psalm Beginning with Two Lines
of Smart's *Jubilate Agno*

For the Lord commanded Moses concerning the cats at
the departure of the Children of Israel from Egypt.
For every family had one cat at least in the bag.
For that is the origin of the phrase "to let the cat out of
the bag"
For cats do not like to travel from their homes in cages,
nor Sherpa bags, nor will they submit to the collar or
the leash.
For all days to the Cat are the Sabbath, the day of rest
and freedom from the yoke.
For the Children of Israel had learned from the
Egyptians the excellence of cats and their fastidious
maintenance.
For lo, even in Herodotus it is written of the Egyptians
that they mourned their cats who had died
For the Egyptians shaved off their eyebrows to remember
a perished feline.
For the bereaved Egyptians must have seemed often
quizzical, with no eyebrows.
For when their dogs died, the Egyptians shaved their
whole bodies as well as their heads, altogether a less
subtle look

For a missing eyebrow would be raised at death, like a
    question mark on its side.
For I do not know if the Egyptians then drew eyebrows
    on over their shaved-off ones, as some ladies do,
    unfortunately, to this day.
For the Egyptians mummified their dead cats, that they
    might prowl the afterlife, stalking mice forever
For the mice were in the afterlife too, even without
    getting mummified, crawling through some wormhole
    in the wainscoting to get at the golden grain left for
    the Pharaohs.
For the cats had their own cat goddess, and were already
    monotheistic.
For cats did not believe in the dog-headed god of Death,
    if you consider a jackal a dog, which I do.
For the cats had little need of an afterlife, in truth, what
    with their nine regular ones.
For when they were mummified, it was in strips of
    papyrus, Egyptian newspaper.
For on this were sometimes the scraps of poems, the
    news that stays news
For cats know how to scan, and make no false quantities.
For cats are poetry, whereas dogs are prose.
For Moses could issue no commandments to the cats
    themselves, for cats only contemplate suggestions.

For a dog moves his tail to say Yes, but the cat moves her
tail to say No.

For the cats told Moses to divide the Red Sea, for they
had a repugnance of getting their paws damp

For the dry sands of Egypt proved an excellent litter box,
and preserver of papyrus

For in some theories, cats carry the parasites of insanity

For the mummies of cats are wrapped in ancient laundry
lists and the lost fragments of Sappho.

For a shaved eyebrow is the lacuna of grief.

The Pull Toy

You squeezed its leash in your fist,
It followed where you led:
Tick, tock, tick, tock,
Nodding its wooden head,

Wagging a tail on a spring,
Its wheels gearing lackety-clack,
Dogging your heels the length of the house,
Though you seldom glanced back.

It didn't mind being dragged
When it toppled on its side
Scraping its coat of primary colors:
Love has no pride.

But now that you run and climb
And leap, it has no hope
Of keeping up, so it sits, hunched
At the end of its rope

And dreams of a rummage sale
Where it's snapped up for a song,
And of somebody—somebody just like you—
Stringing it along.

Refugee Fugue

1.

AEGEAN BLUES

The sea is for holidaymakers, summer on the beach,
Surely there is space enough to spread a towel for each;
Dry land isn't something you should pray to reach.

Look how glad our kids are, making their sandy town,
And how they build the battlements the laughing waves
    tear down.
But it's the selfsame water, where some swim, and others
    drown.

The sea is full of dangers, the shallows and the deep.
The sea is full of treasures, down there five fathoms deep,
The sea is full of salt: there are no more tears to weep.

The ferryman says we cross tonight; and everyone pays
    cash.
Charon don't take Mastercard, you have to pay him cash.
The water seems so calm tonight, you hardly hear the
    splash.

There was a boy named Icarus; old Daedalus's son.
He turned into a waxwing, black against the sun.
Drowned because he tried to fly. (He's not the only one.)

Why would a kid lie in the sand, and not take off his shoes?
Why would he lie there facedown, the color of a bruise?
The sea can make you carefree, nothing left to lose.

There's indigo and turquoise, there's cobalt, sapphire, navy,
And there's a dark like wine, my love, out where things get
    wavy.
Listen, that's the worry note, reminds me of my baby.

2.

CHARON

When some, as promised, made it to dry land,
He profited, high and dry, but others, owing
To fickle winds, or a puncture, or freak waves,
Arrived at a farther shore, another beach
Lapped by a numb forgetting, still in the clothes
Someone had washed and pressed to face the day,
And lay in attitudes much like repose.
And Charon made a killing either way,
Per child alone, 600 euros each.

3

AEGEAN EPIGRAMS

We beheld the Aegean blossoming with bodies.
—Aeschylus, *Agamemnon*

Upon an unseaworthy wooden vessel

Call it a tub, call it a casket.
(And all their eggs tucked in this basket.)

The woman from Leros

The woman from Leros said:
"Small bodies wash ashore,
Sea-chewed, a few days dead.
I don't eat fish anymore."

From an autopsy report of an unknown drowning victim, Ikaria

Female. Nine years old. Found wearing a blouse
And a pair of sweatpants patched with Minnie Mouse.

Duties

Which one seems more chilling:
Copenhagen willing
To confiscate cash and bauble

From Mosul, Homs, and Kabul;
Or smugglers making a killing
Palming Charon's obol?

Fathomless

A fathom deep, the body lies, beyond all helps and harms,
Unfathomable, unfathomable, the news repeats, like charms,
Forgetting that "to fathom" is to hold within your arms.

Word problem

The 21-foot-long dinghy can hold up to 30 people, max.
If you squeeze on 64, wave a 9 millimeter at their backs,
In 6 Beaufort, 2 nautical miles out into international waters,
Which do you not save first—infants, sons, mothers, fathers,
    daughters?

Paradox

Of the ones that happened to die, the little ones and the old,
By hypothermia, or drowning, all died of cold.

Nothing to declare

As if in a sea of red tape
The faulty life jackets tossed:
There is no customhouse, no guards,
At the border these have crossed.

Proposed epitaph for drowned refugee children

Go tell the bureaucrats, passerby, that all is shipshape, fine.
The stuff that trickles from your eye is only a little brine.

4.

APPENDIX A: USEFUL PHRASES IN
ARABIC, FARSI/DARI, AND GREEK

(found poem, from the Guide to Volunteering
in Athens, *as updated for March 17, 2016)*

Welcome to Greece!

Thank God for your safe arrival (greeting after trip)

Hello

Good morning

Good evening

Good night

Thank you

You're welcome

Please

I don't understand

I don't speak Arabic / Farsi

Slowly

Come here

You're safe

Are you wet / cold?

Yes / No

My name is . . .

What is your name?

He / She / It is

We / They are

God is with the patient (will make people laugh)

Give yourself a break (comforting words)

Free (no charge)

Refugee

Volunteer

Foreigner

Friend

I am hungry

Thirsty

Food

Water

Does it hurt?

Sick

Pregnant

Mother / Father

Brother / Sister

Child

Family

What country is your family from?

Pharmacy

Medicine

Hospital

Doctor

Tent

Sorry, it has run out

We do not have it now

New shoes only if yours are broken

Wait here, please

I will return soon

Follow me / Come with me

Come back in . . .

5 / 15 / 45 minutes

One hour

Quarter / Half hour / Half day

Today / Tomorrow / Yesterday

How many people?

Sorry

Stay calm

One line, please

Next person

The Rosehead Nail

Blacksmithing demonstration, Monteagle, Tennessee

"But can you forge a nail?" the pale boy asks,
And the blacksmith shoves a length of iron rod
Deep in the coal fire cherished by the bellows
Until it glows volcanic. He was a god
Before anachronism, before the tasks
That had been craft were jobbed out to machine.
By dint of hammer-song he makes his keen,
Raw point, and crowns utility with rose:
Quincunx of facets petaling its head.
The breeze-made-visible sidewinds. The boy's
Blonde mother shifts and coughs. *Once Work was wed
To Loveliness*—sweat-faced, swarthy from soot, he
Reminds us with the old saw he employs
(And doesn't miss a beat): "Smoke follows beauty."

The Sabine Women

O Ravishers, O Husbands, you have won:
We are the country that is tamed by children.
Light-footed maidens now waddle behind
Bellies in which two histories quicken the future.
Tomorrow will dawn with a pang, like breaking waters.
Oh you have yoked us, yes, but you have yoked
Us to yourselves—now, see, you too are bounded
On all sides not by enemies but in-laws.
A sigh has turned the heart into a hearth:
Let marriage be a truce—for from now on
The war between us is a civil war.

Scissors

Are singular, and plural, un-
Canny: *one plus one is one*;

Even in solitude, a pair,
Cheek to cheek, or on a tear,

Knives at cross-purposes, bereaving
Cleavers to each other cleaving:

Open, shut; give and take,
All dichotomy in their wake.

What starts with sighs, concludes in "or"s:
His or hers; mine or yours:

Divvy up. Slice clean, slice deep,
In pinked jags, or one swift sweep,

The crisp sheet where they met and married,
The paper where the blades are buried.

Sea Urchins

The sea urchins star
the seafloor like sunken mines
from a rust-smirched war

filmed in black and white.
Or if they are stars they are
negatives of light,

their blind beams brittle
purple needles with no eyes:
not even spittle

and a squint will thread
the sea's indigo ribbons.
We float overhead

like angels, or whales,
with our soft underbellies
just beyond their pales,

their dirks and rankles.
Nothing is bare as bare feet,
naked as ankles.

They whisker their risks
in the fine print of footnotes'
irksome asterisks.

Their extraneous
complaints are lodged with dark dots,
subcutaneous

ellipses . . . seizers
seldom extract even with
olive oil, tweezers.

Sun-bleached, they unclench
their sharps, doom scalps their hackles,
unbuttons their stench.

Their shells are embossed
and beautiful calculus,
studded turbans, tossed

among drummed pebbles
and plastic flotsam—so smooth,
so fragile, baubles

like mermaid doubloons,
these rose-, mauve-, pistachio-
tinted macaroons.

Selvage

(from self + edge, *the firmly woven edge*
of a fabric that resists unraveling)

(ODYSSEY, 22.468–473)

Who knew her son had salvaged so many hates?
Their feet twitched a little, like thrushes caught
In a fowler's net. The simile had the tang
Of remorse. No, surely the idea was his
To hoist them up like flags in their long skirts,
Modest now, the sluts, the dirty flirts,
Tongueless belles, spinsters of their own doom.
While they twitched, a flutter of pity. But as it is
She finds them tidy and domesticated,
Dull plumaged with death, now that they hang,
As if in the spotlit vitrine of a future museum,
From the warp like a dozen ancient loom weights.

Shattered

Another smashed glass,
wrong end of a gauche gesture
towards a cliff—compass-

rose of mis-direc-
tions, scattered to the twelve winds,
the wine-dark sea wreck.

Wholeness won't stay put.
Why these sweeping conclusions?
Always you're barefoot,

nude-soled in a room
fanged with recriminations,
leaning on a broom.

How can you know what's
missing, unless you puzzle
all the shards? What cuts

is what's overlooked,
the sliver of the unseen,
faceted, edged, hooked,

unremarked atom
of remorse broadcast across
lame linoleum.

Archaeologist
of the just-made mistake, sift
smithereens of schist

for the unhidden
right-in-plain-sight needling
mote in the midden.

Fragments, say your feet,
make the shivered, shimmering
brokenness complete.

Shoulda, Woulda, Coulda

The mood made him tense—
How she sharpened conditional futures
On strops of might-have-beens,
The butchered present in sutures.

He cursed in the fricative,
The way she could not act.
Or live in the indicative,
Only contrary to fact.

Tomorrow should have been vast,
Bud-packed, grenade-gravid,
Not just a die miscast.

It made him sad, it made him livid:
How she construed from the imperfect past
A future less vivid.

Silence

Silence has its own notation: dark
Jottings of duration, but not pitch,
A long black box, or little feathered hitch
Like a new Greek letter or diacritical mark.
Silence is a function of Time, the lark
In flight but not in song. A nothing which
Keeps secrets or confesses. Pregnant, rich,
Or awkward, cold, the pause that makes us hark,
The space before or after: it's the room
In which melody moves, the medium
Through which thought travels, it is golden, best,
Welcome relief to talk-worn tedium.
Before the word itself, it was the womb.
It has a measure. Music calls it rest.

Similes, Suitors

Odyssey

1. BOOK CHI

Just as an illegal haul of undersized mullet
Is heaved out of the overfished Aegean
(Many-sounding, white-maned, dark as wine)
And dumped out hugger-mugger on the shingle
Midst plastic bottle caps and the mirthless laughter
Of seagulls lured by biodegradation,
And leaving behind no fingerling nurseries,
Just so the bodies of the suitors lay
Dumb and twitching in a heap, a school
Of gape-mouthed, goggle-eyed incomprehension
Gasping for breath out in their foreseeable doom
In the paparazzi-flash of solar flare
Dead to the future generations, grieving
For the lost current, for the swim of things.

The suitors' skittish shades began to squeak
Like the scritch of a toxic-fumed permanent marker
Scratching off the names of those who are absent,
Or as when deep in a cave, a small brown bat
Plummets to the guano-spackled basement
Jagged with assorted speleothems
And the colony of bats is all a-twitter,
A roost that's been afflicted with the fungus
That causes the contagious white-nose syndrome
Which strikes during hibernation, rousing the bats
From torpor early, stirring them to starve,
And they gibber like dementia from the cave's mouth
Into the starless, cold night of extinction,
Taking with them a white night-blooming flower
Dependent on chiropterophily,
Just so the suitors pipistrelled and bleeped,
Trailing the lord of florists, with his wand
And Nike sandals, He who delivers a species
Like a bouquet of spiky asphodel,
Apalled with pollen, to the halls of Hell.

Sounion

You shouldn't wait for signs out on a cliff
Watching the razzle-dazzle of the water
If you've no head for heights. Go home, and say
You only saw three half-tame partridges
Among the rocks, and a seagull in the distance
That seemed at first like the shake of a white sheet.
If news is good, you cannot hurry it;
If news is bad, it tracks you down. Don't meet
Catastrophe halfway, the steep *what if*.
The offing's full of optical illusions:
The sails are black, but don't jump to conclusions.

The Stain

Remembers
Your embarrassment,
Wine or blood,
Sweat or oil,

When the ink leaked
Your intent
Because you thought
No truth could soil,

Or when you let
The secret slip,
Or when you dropped
The leaden hint,

Or when between
The cup and lip,
The Beaujolais
Pled innocent,

Or when the rumor's
Fleet was launched,
Or when the sheets
Waged their surrender,

But the breach
Could not be staunched
And no apology
Would tender;

When over-served,
You misconstrued
And blurbed your heartsick
On your sleeve,

When everything
Became imbued
With sadness, yet
You couldn't grieve.

Inalienable
As DNA,
Self-evident
As fingerprints,

It will not out
Although you spray
And presoak in the sink
And rinse:

What they suspect
The stain will know,
The stain records
What you forget.

If you wear it,
It will show;
If you wash it,
It will set.

Summer Birthdays

You would learn in kindergarten
There was one game you had no part in:
Kings and queens of endless noons—
You envied them their golden rule
In crowns of bright construction paper—
The cupcakes, streamers, brave balloons,
The breath and the expiring taper.
Later there were those at school

Whose invitation list would pique
The class's interest for a week:
Sleepovers where all was said,
Or giggled, about *who* liked *whom*,
And anyone who left the room
Would have only herself to thank
As butt of some unfunny prank.
Sleep sneaked in at dawn. Instead

You always seemed to be at camp
Slouched on a picnic bench still damp
From swimsuit bottoms—next to one,
Your brief, best, only friend for three

Long weeks of forced hilarity—
Arts and crafts and nature fun.
You stared down at your ugly sandals
Hating the song and the stupid candles.

In the dog days, playing dead,
There still lies a sense of dread—
Something in you that accrues
As you watch the summer blaze
Through the cyclopean days—
The wine-dark sea of summer blues,
Fierce skies extinguished one by one
When the dusk blows out the sun.

Most everything you love was born
At the cusp of harvest-time
When the year was in its prime,
Before the autumn winds had torn
The turning pages from the trees
And rent the spider's thread of pride
And brought the flowers to their knees.
Every summer, like a tide

The anniversaries arrive
Un-clockwise, with the clockwork earth:

Sister, mother, daughter, son,
Yourself—and then the other one,
Your father, were he still alive:
Every August, you have cried
When you celebrate his birth
Ten days after he has died.

And maybe it's not only Dad—
But summer too, its vague alarm,
Another gone year's epitaph.
The year still seems to start with school—
Fresh pencils, new hopes to be cool—
While summer evenings, late and sad,
End violet and moist and warm
And fading, like a mimeograph.

Sunset, Wings

Crows descry the sky,
desecrate the cyanic,
scrying and crying.

Swallows, I swear, not
swifts; but swift—swoop, swivel—whose
scissored silhouettes,

belated, become
a quibble of pipistrelles,
tippling acrobats.

Who haunts the hill? Lo,
one-note woe: oh well, twilight
throws in the towel.

Swallows

Every year the swallows come
And put their homestead in repair,
And raise another brood, and skim
And boomerang through summer air,
And reap mosquitoes from the hum
Of holidays. A handsome pair,
One on the nest, one on the wire,
Cheat-cheat-cheat, the two conspire

To murder half the insect race,
And feed them squirming to their chicks.
They work and fret at such a pace,
And natter in between, with clicks
And churrs, they lift the raftered place
(Seaside taverna) with their tricks
Of cursive loops and Morse-code call,
Both analog and digital.

They seem to us so coupled, married,
So flustered with their needful young,
So busy housekeeping, so harried,
It's hard to picture them among

The origins of myth—a buried
Secret, rape, a cut-out tongue,
Two sisters wronged, where there's no right,
Till transformation fledges flight.

But Ovid swapped them in the tale,
So that the sister who was forced
Becomes instead the nightingale,
Who sings as though her heart would burst.
It's Ovid's stories that prevail.
And thus the swallow is divorced
Twice from her voice, her tuneless chatter,
And no one asks her what's the matter.

These swallows, though, don't have the knack
For sorrow—or we'd not have guessed—
Though smartly dressed in tailored black,
Spend no time mourning, do not rest,
One scissors forth, one zigzags back,
They take turns settled on the nest
Or waiting on a perch nearby
To zero in on wasp or fly.

They have no time for tragic song,
As dusk distills, they dart and flicker,

The days are long, but not as long
As yesterday. The night comes quicker,
And soon the season will be wrong.
Knackered, cross, they bitch and bicker,
Like you and me. They never learn.
And every summer, they return.

Variation on a Theme by Ouranis

("I shall die on a mournful autumn evening")

I shall die on an October afternoon
Under scumbled skies of verdigris
In Athens, listening to an out-of-tune
Accordion from the street—an old reprise

Of "S'agapó"—just as when we first came
And rented a freezing flat on a steep hill,
And the same accordionist singing the same
Refrain, would pass beneath the windowsill

At the same time every day. You could set the clock
By his voice, and how it told the exilic hour,
And the urge to weep hit like an aftershock,
And grief would edge the tongue like something sour.

Though Tuesday's unlucky, I think that it will be
A Monday when the summons comes from heaven.
For the statistician's daughter, you'll agree,
The chances are pretty good, one out of seven,

128

And Monday's when the farmers' market comes
With the shaggy roots of things pried from the ground,
And olives black and blue as hammered thumbs,
Oblong, and shriveled, or compact, fat and round.

Whatever you might need, our neighborhood handles.
Next door, next to the butcher and the baker,
And the paraffin shop that makes the votive candles,
Is the going concern of an undertaker.

And we're just five blocks from the First Cemetery,
Though it would take more influence than we've got
To get me in. I suppose they'd have to bury
Me with the foreigners, if I could get a plot.

My burial shall be unorthodox,
Though I don't mind the chants and undertones,
Not being embalmed, dropped down in a plain box.
And three years later, they'll dig up my bones.

Whethering

The rain is haunted;
I had forgotten.
My children are two hours abed
And yet I rise
Hearing behind the typing of the rain,

Its abacus and digits,
A voice calling me again,
Softer, clearer.
The kids lie buried under duvets, sound
Asleep. It isn't them I hear, it's

Something formless that fidgets
Beyond the window's benighted mirror,
Where a negative develops, where reflection
Holds up a glass of spirits.
White noise

Precipitates.
Rain is a kind of recollection.
Much has been shed,
Hissing indignantly into the ground.
It is the listening

Belates,

Haunted by these finger taps and sighs

Behind the beaded-curtain glistening,

As though by choices that we didn't make and never wanted,

As though by the dead and misbegotten.

Acknowledgments

Able Muse: "The Myrtle Grove" (first sonnet)

American Life in Poetry: "The Pull Toy"

Ash: "Little Owl"

The Atlantic: "Ajar," "Pencil," "Sunset, Wings"

The Battersea Review: "Pandora"

Beloit Poetry Journal: "Lost and Found," "Selvage"

The Dark Horse: "Psalm Beginning with
Two Lines of Smart's *Jubilate Agno*," "Scissors"

Five Points: "Cast Irony," "For Atalanta," "The Pull Toy,"
"The Sabine Women," "Summer Birthdays"

The Hampden-Sydney Poetry Review: "Silence"

Harvard Review: "Shattered"

Image: "Cyprian Variations"

Light: "Glitter"

Literary Matters: "Dyeing the Easter Eggs," "Empathy"

The Nation: "Sea Urchins"

135

The New Criterion: "Denouement," "The Stain"

The New Yorker: "Shoulda, Woulda, Coulda," "Swallows"

The New York Review of Books: "Placebo"

Octopus Magazine: "Similes, Suitors" (Book Omega)

Oxford American: "The Erstwhile Archivist"
(as "The Summer Archivist")

Oxford Poetry: "Variation on a Theme by Ouranis"

Parnassus: Poetry in Review: "Art Monster" (the phrase
"art monster" was popularized by Jenny Offill in
Dept. of Speculation), "The Mycenaean Bridge"

Poetry: "After a Greek Proverb," "The Companions
of Odysseus in Hades," "Epic Simile," "First
Miracle," "Like, the Sestina" (as "Sestina, Like"),
"Momentary," "The Rosehead Nail," "Whethering"

The Poetry Review: "Battle of Plataea: Aftermath"
(as "Aftermath: Battle of Plataea"), "The Last Carousel"

Resistance, Rebellion, Life: 50 Poems Now:
Portions of "Refugee Fugue"

The Sewanee Review: "Dutch Flower Painting
from the 1670s," "Lice," "Peacock Feathers"

The Spectator: "Parmenion"

Subtropics: "Crow, Gentleman"
(as "Gentleman Crow"), "Autumn Pruning"

32 Poems: "Night Thoughts"

TLS: "Half of an Epic Simile Not Found
in Hesiod," "Memorial (*Mnemosyno*)"

Unsplendid: "Bedbugs in Marriage Bed," "Sounion"

Virginia Quarterly Review: "Alice, Bewildered,"
"Colony Collapse Disorder"

With gratitude to the Guggenheim Foundation, United States Artists, and the MacArthur Foundation for their generous support.

And thanks always to John Psaropoulos, stalwart first reader, and to Ben Folit-Weinberg, Chris Childers, Dick Davis, Jonathan Galassi, Rachel Hadas, Mike Levine, Ange Mlinko, and Catherine Tufariello for their keen eyes, ears, and advice.

Thank you to the editors of the *Best American Poetry* series for selecting "Ajar," "Alice, Bewildered," "Pencil," and "Shattered."

And to Poetry Daily for featuring "Colony Collapse Disorder," "Crow, Gentleman," and "Selvage."

Ευχαριστώ also to the festival Cyprus—Literary Destination for inspiring "Cyprian Variations."